AMONG DEAD THINGS

poems by

Celia Lawren

Finishing Line Press
Georgetown, Kentucky

AMONG DEAD THINGS

Copyright © 2020 by Celia Lawren
ISBN 978-1-64662-170-5 First Edition
All rights reserved under International and Pan-American Copyright Conventions. No part of this book may be reproduced in any manner whatsoever without written permission from the publisher, except in the case of brief quotations embodied in critical articles and reviews.

ACKNOWLEDGMENTS

Cæsura: Bounty
Tule Review: Waiting for my daughter to come home

Publisher: Leah Maines

Editor: Christen Kincaid

Cover Art: JoAnn Ugolini, *between spaces 1*

Author Photo: Diane McLean

Cover Design: Elizabeth Maines McCleavy

Printed in the USA on acid-free paper.
Order online: www.finishinglinepress.com
       also available on amazon.com

           Author inquiries and mail orders:
                 Finishing Line Press
                   P. O. Box 1626
            Georgetown, Kentucky 40324
                    U. S. A.

Table of Contents

Legacy of Losses 1

One

My daughter lies in ICU Bay #2 5

The Work of Angels 6

Courtroom dream after sentencing 8

Home briefly from my daughter's bedside 9

Worst Nightmare 10

Entering Worlds 12

Two

Prison Visitations 15

On desolate days, I think of Portland and Peter 16

A heart can beat, separate even from the body 17

Waiting for my daughter to come home 18

Scale 19

Bounty 20

To keep alive among the dead things she carries 21

The day my daughter walks 22

> *Once there was a shock*
> *that left behind a long, shimmering comet tail.*
> *It keeps us inside. It makes the TV pictures snowy.*
> *It settles in cold drops on the telephone wires.*
>
> —Tomas Tranströmer
> *After a Death, The Half-Finished Heaven*

Legacy of Losses

It starts with a snip of the cord.
A childhood friend moves away.
Another friend survives chemo,
marrow transplants,
only to die, exhausted,
of the osteosarcoma.
Your high school boyfriend takes
his emerald class ring from your neck,
looks back apologetically.
Your husband walks out the door,
never looks back.
Losses accumulate
like stacks of dirty dishes.
There's nothing to do
but stand at the sink,
wash each one,
and place it in the rack.
One morning, I found
our black lab sprawled
on the cold basement slab,
a hulk of a dog who once slipped
one paw after another
into the soapy water
until all of him was in
my young daughter's bath.
I told the vet, *just take him,*
then watched my daughter
chew the news into her jaw.
She taped his photo to the fridge.
I heard her throat catch
each time she opened the door.

One

My daughter lies in ICU Bay #2

head thrashing,
ravaging a bloodied pillow.
She pulls at tubes
like a trapped animal
tearing at a net.
Severe head trauma,
the doctor tells me.
On her face—not one scratch,
though lungs and kidneys are punctured,
arms, legs, and pelvis broken.
Miracle, nurses whisper, as
they empty bags of urine,
search for good veins,
turn her over like a sack of rice.
I pick slivers of windshield
from her mat of gold hair
grateful just to touch her.
At night, I sink into fractured dreams,
the dead woman tells me,
from now on, nothing is gonna be right.

The Work of Angels

For the tombstone of his beloved wife Emelyn,
sculptor William Story cuts his sorrow deep
into the heart of the marble
until the angel collapses,
muffles her cries in a cradled arm,
feathered wings folded around her.

    x

Sirens howl, emergency vehicles surround
two smoldering cars locked head-on.
An Accord is folded around a man and woman
whose bloodied faces stare blankly down the road.
In a Corolla, a woman sits crushed
in a web of windshield and steel.
First responders work the Jaws of Life.

    x

This scene plays over and over in my head.
Does an angel, wings like heartbeats,
whisper beneath the neon flashers:
now this one goes to the light,
now this one stays in the darkness?

    x

I make my way to the Protestant Cemetery
in Rome, crowded with the bones
of artists and literary elites
the likes of Percy and Mary Shelley, Keats.
There, among rows of mildewed monuments, is Story's
The Angel of Grief Weeping Over the Dismantled Altar of Life:
"the pain of those left behind," he wrote.
Smaller than I imagined, the angel tired of weeping,
the statue is Story's last. He died one year past his wife.

x

How heavy human souls must be to ferry.
How heavy the grief of an angel.

Courtroom dream after daughter's sentencing

as a man in black enters the room, the characters stand—except the woman in a wheelchair who can't. a dude holds a surfboard, ready to ride a wave out of there. another man, painted gray with a heavy accent, is mumbling & stooped over. an angry young woman shouts, "murder, murder!" and the prosecutor recites evidential facts with no sympathetic comprehension, but good diction; he's full of ambition. a young girl comes forward holding a drawing of her dead mother: *how sad she is to grow up without her.* everyone cries. the angry woman keeps yelling, "murder, murder. it's not fair she's alive." the woman in the wheelchair is sobbing, her mouth covered with duct tape. i appear next to her, patting her shoulder, repeating, "but she is good. she is good. please, she is good." the guard calls out sternly, "No touching," but i do anyway. the judge shakes his head sadly, says he must split the baby. the woman in the wheelchair is pushed offstage into prison. the surfer dude says he did all he could & high-fives his way out. i didn't know what to make of the scene, such a fucked-up story. i knew, halfway through, it wouldn't end well for any of them.

Home briefly from my daughter's bedside

Sleepless, I walk the familiar
path along the creek, air heavy
with early morning mist,
past two scarred persimmons
burdened with overripe fruit.
At the bend, tall grasses
 lay crushed, the imprint of a buck.
I want to lie down next to
the animal's furred body,
press my face against his.
But the vision fades into sunlight.
All I see is trampled green,
tangled stems scattered.
Back at the hospital,
police guard my daughter's door
as if she could walk out.
What can I tell her?

Worst Nightmare

Late sun glistened on the ocean like thousands of lit sparklers as the students gathered on the restaurant patio to celebrate. Easy laughter floated like notes from a gospel choir. Proud they'd made it through the string of lousy part-time jobs, being robbed or felt-up at parties, acquiring the requisite classes to graduate on time, they were at the threshold of big change. What they wanted, had worked hard for, was so close they could taste it in the nachos and margarita mix.

x

Shards and broken threads pieced together of that night, of which Brianna has no recollection…There was a celebration of college graduation. A plan to sleep over at a girlfriend's apartment changed as the evening progressed. The girlfriend left, Brianna stayed, the boyfriend called, demanding she come home. She was drunk & lost, calling for directions. Freeway entry under construction, she drove the other way, headlong into an oncoming car carrying a couple on their casino date night. The woman in the headlong car was killed in the collision.

x

After 24 hours, the boyfriend called her best friend for help, called every hospital. The next day, they called again, asking for Jane Does. They found her in an ICU in swanky La Jolla. The CHP took her ID, didn't give the hospital her name or notify next of kin.

x

I wake again and again. I want dreams that are different than this.

x

Brianna's refused bail, is in county jail 500 miles away, in a wheelchair, wearing arm and leg casts due off six weeks ago. Behind the pane of glass, I try to make out what she slurs over and over. "My arm, on fire." I call her lawyer. *Get her out.*

Entering worlds

Like a miniature Gertrude Ederle
crossing the English Channel,
Brianna freestyled the birth canal
one month early.
When her downy cap burst through,
she let out a victory cry prematurely.
My body would not let her go.
Maybe premonition told me
to keep her in the womb—not relinquish her
to a world where fireflies fade into extinction.
A mother knows how easy it can be
to slip from one world into another,
to be pulled under, suddenly find yourself
deep in the ocean where millions of miles
of earth's guts spill out: an open wound
that never heals.

Two

Prison Visitations

Number 5790217 squats
for a cavity search
behind the far wall,
then emerges—
my daughter smiling.
I've arrived early
for the entry queue
carrying the allowable
number of quarters
for vending machines.
We sit at shared tables
careful not to let our lunch
spill over the boundaries of
our balkanized slice of space.
Brianna feasts on favorites—fried spring rolls,
fresh strawberries, hot chocolate,
devours the details of my daily life.
I look around. Children fight
to sit on their mothers' laps.
Couples steal kisses. Old-timers,
faces carved by disappointment and deceit,
fawn over babies. Younger inmates flirt
with guards who slipped them
a latex-gloved finger on the way in.
The bell rings and we head
to the sign-out line holding hands.
I'll call you Monday, she whispers.

On desolate days, I think of Portland and Peter

waiting with his walking stick
to begin the tour.
As he turns to greet us, I notice
his hearing aid, his half a nose,
like a plastic model cutaway,
only his stiff cartilage, tomato red.
Crossing 3rd Ave by the Dekum Building,
he proudly confides he's just completed
training as a sightseeing guide
at the School for the Blind.
Having marched across the Sahara
with the British over land mines,
he's adept at counting steps,
something I just realize.
Still, he is impressive,
towering over passersby
in Pioneer Courthouse Square,
long muscular legs in walking shorts,
a sonorous voice, perfect Queen's English.
We stop at the corner of SW 5th Ave
and Taylor, where Peter describes a curious sculpture—
a coyote carrying objects on its back.
"This is the Native American trickster coyote,
representing life out of balance," he says.
"The bird is the killdeer and the salmon—
which you know give up their lives to have children—
depict the struggles of parenthood."
I look down at the plaque:
The Responsibility of Raising a Child.
Joan says, "What a reminder to have on a sidewalk."
David asks, "Who is the person on the coyote?"
Peter answers, "That's the matriarch,
the one typically in tribal culture
who puts lives back in balance."

A heart can beat, separate even from the body

In those early years, my daughter new to prison,
when I cried out, a baby wanting,
out of the blue, on the phone, at night alone,
I reminded myself, *no one dies of a broken heart.*
The heart beats 80 times a minute, 42,048,000 times a year.
You have seven years to go, I'd say.
When this person or that in the prison administration
denied her pain meds, request for a second mattress,
as thin as a nylon slip, to help cushion the metal
securing her body, and when, by accident,
she touched a guard's arm and they threw her in solitary,
I scolded, *you've got to pace yourself.* I've read
the blood vessel system wraps two times around the earth.

Waiting for my daughter to come home

God knows, I didn't want *my* mother
to return from the dead.
Still, the clothes I took of hers
hung unworn eleven years
before I took them to Goodwill.
Now I stand in front of your closet
grieving, as if you had died,
and breathe in the faint nectar
of J-Lo's Glow and your special shampoo
for honey blondes.
They say smell is the oldest sense.
Like a fingerprint, we carry our own.
My mother's was wild fennel on a cold wind.
They say you can smell fear
in a person's sweat. But what of loss?
How many years
will these clothes hang limp?
The gold lace for your cousin's wedding,
the black-hooded goth number you wore at junior prom.
I draw them to my face.
I'm like the Gee's Bend quilter Missouri Petway,
who gathered up her dead husband's faded denim,
the smell of Mississippi Delta red clay and grease,
tore the pant legs and shirttails into long
rectangular pieces the shape of his body,
then stitched them together in a quilt
and buried herself every night underneath it.

Scale

When a friend asks me,
How do you do it?
You seem fine,
I want to agree.
I want to feel
nothing's changed,
take comfort in the
solidity of that.
But I know sometime today—
and every day—
I'll retrieve
the scale of justice
from the kitchen closet
and carefully place it
on the table
to balance
my daughter's losses
against another's.
Weighing loss
against loss,
grief against grief,
is heavy, surely
as heavy as
the sinking sea floor,
one side to the other,
a place to hide
in silence.

Bounty

Saturday morning at the farmer's market.
I thump the bellies of watermelons,
succumb to peachy sweetness,
cradle one fuzzy butt like a baby's.
Another summer, and my daughter's still in prison,
surviving like a seedling stuck in a Dixie cup.
There's no harvest in California lock-up,
only canned meat, potato buds,
meals pumped with starchy filler.
Summer is the stench
of feed lot cattle stalled in still air,
a merciless sun beating down on bodies
corralled behind barbed wire,
grit caught in cracked lips.
There, fields yield stones
plowed under. And here I am,
crying over one rosy peach
bruised in my hand.

To keep alive among the dead things she carries

my spirit flies to my daughter's closet-size prison cell at night, sometimes to stand guard,
sometimes to stroke her long golden hair. spirit sees the remains of my daughter's dreams
lying on the cold concrete floor, crushed like a million monarch butterflies free-fallen
in a flash freeze, soft crackling underfoot, a memory. she moves her wings slowly,
gathering the delicate pieces—fuzzy thoraxes, soft underbellies, wisps of hindwings
and forewings, tiny legs like eyelashes, pinheads with their bulging eyes & all-seeing antennae.
spirit refashions the parts, returns them to glistening chrysalises, suspended, waiting
for my daughter.

The day my daughter walks

she is 2 months past 30, 8 years after
the start of her sentence;
her prior record: one run stop sign.

In brand new street clothes,
she emerges from the guard station,
begins the 40 steps to the waiting car.
She moves in slow motion,
as if weighted by the drag
of the godforsaken,
those terrifying Killing Trees
that clutch at humans fleeing hell
in Dante's *Inferno*.

She's at the metal gate.
As it slides, the bottom grates
against the concrete, screeching
acuminously. I hold my breath,
not daring to shift the tilt of the planet
and cause the gate to close
before she can slip through.

Celia Lawren was born in 1949 in a small town in Florida. She received her BA in Spanish and Classical Humanities and MS in Environmental Management from Florida State University, somehow avoiding any English courses. For the next decade, she worked in the environmental field in Washington DC and California before switching to a career in marketing in Silicon Valley. In 2002, when she formed her own marketing communications company, she joined a creative writing group and fell in love with poetry. She now lives in Knoxville, Tennessee and has two grown children and one granddaughter who reside in California.

www.ingramcontent.com/pod-product-compliance
Lightning Source LLC
LaVergne TN
LVHW041521070426
835507LV00012B/1732